why does my mom call me mouse?

tracy m schmidt

WestBow Press books may be ordered through booksellers or by contacting:

WestBow Press
A Division of Thomas Nelson & Zondervan
1663 Liberty Drive
Bloomington, IN 47403
www.westbowpress.com
844-714-3454

Illustrations by Tracy Schmidt.

ISBN: 979-8-3850-2047-8 (sc)
ISBN: 979-8-3850-2048-5 (hc)
ISBN: 979-8-3850-2049-2 (e)

Library of Congress Control Number: 2024904460

Print information available on the last page.

WestBow Press rev. date: 7/10/2024

WESTBOW
P R E S S®
A DIVISION OF THOMAS NELSON
& ZONDERVAN

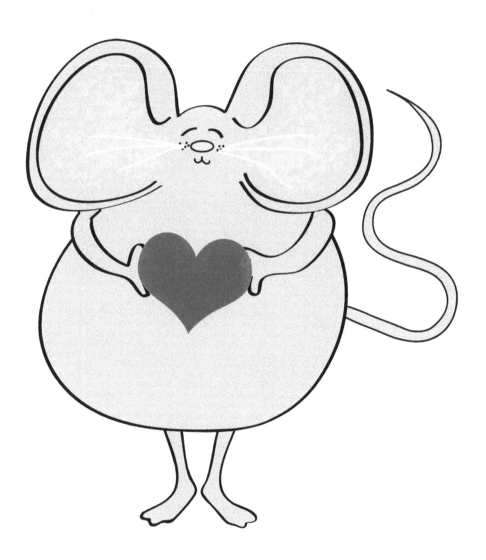

 **when** I was a newborn, my mom carried me home from the hospital in her arms. I was the baby in the family. She named me Tracy Michele, but my mom almost always called me Mouse!

Welcome to the World! Mouse!

even as I was growing up, my mom still called me Mouse! On my fourth birthday, she made me a cake in the shape of a mouse. It had cupcake ears, a pink gumdrop nose, a big red jujube candy heart for its eye, and a smile made of red liquorice. My mom sprinkled pink coconut flakes on the icing to make it look furry, just like a real mouse. My gift was a cuddly mouse plush toy with a long curly tail!

when I was five years old, I started school. My school was across the street from my house. My mom would hold my hand as we crossed the road. She would wave goodbye to me and say, "Have a good day at school, Mouse!"

as I got older, I began to wonder why my mom called me Mouse. I was much bigger than a mouse! *Do I look like a mouse? I wondered. Are my ears fluffy, round, and pink like a mouse?* I looked at my ears in the mirror. No, they didn't look like mouse ears at all!

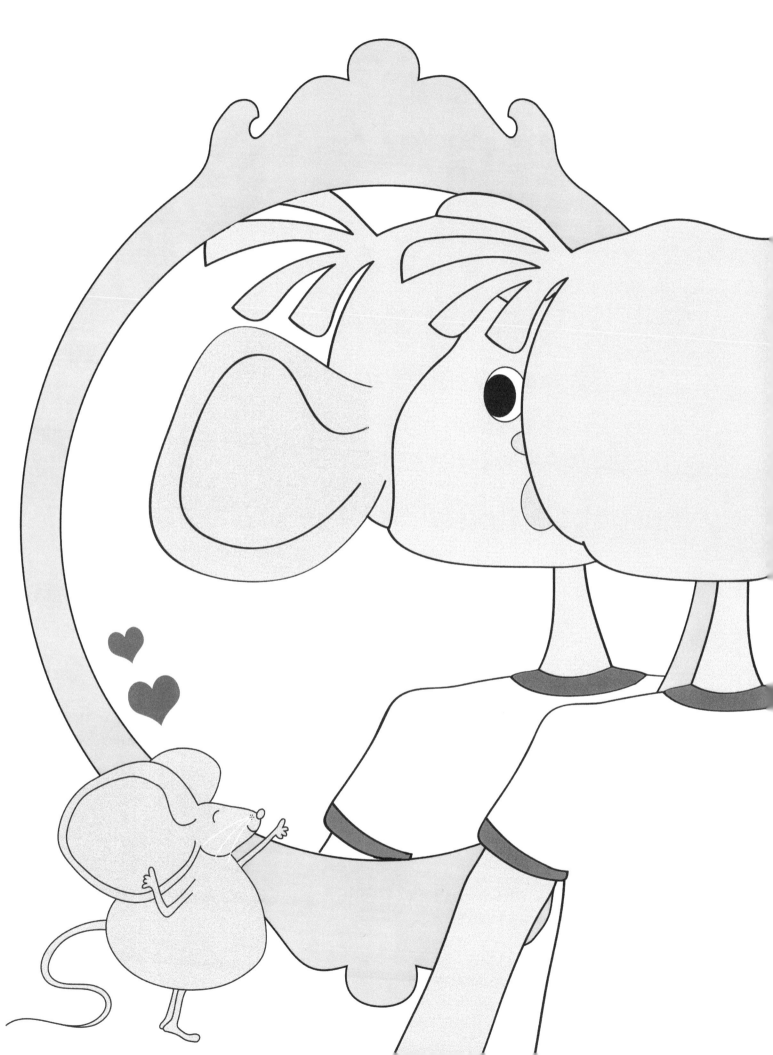

maybe I had a long, pointy pink nose like a mouse. I looked at my nose in the mirror. No, it didn't look like a mouse nose at all!

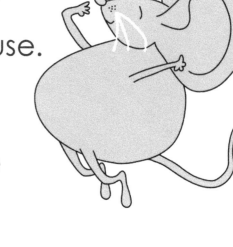

Do I have whiskers growing from my cheeks? I thought. I looked in the mirror. No, no whiskers!

I knew a mouse had fur. Sometimes a mouse had gray fur, brown fur, or even white fur. I was pretty sure I had hair not fur, and my hair wasn't gray, brown, or white; it was blond! I looked in the mirror just to make sure. Yes, I was right! I had wavy yellow hair and no fur at all.

could I possibly have a long tail like a mouse? No, that couldn't be! Just to double-check, I twisted around and looked in the mirror. No, there was no tail that I could see!

maybe, I thought, *it is because I love to eat* cheese. A mouse loves to nibble on cheese too. So I didn't eat cheese for three whole days, but my mom still called me Mouse!

then I figured it out! My mom called me Mouse because when I ran around the house, I was as quiet as a mouse! So the next time I ran past my mom, I made a loud stomping noise with my feet. Now she couldn't call me Mouse anymore, but she did! I had to think some more.

the next day when I came home from school, I went to my bedroom to change out of my uniform. I saw a pretty purple box on top of my bed. My mom came into my room and sat on the bed beside me. She opened the box and pulled out a fuzzy pink blanket and a picture of a newborn baby.

"**this** is the blanket I wrapped you in when you were only a few days old," my mom told me. "I brought you home from the hospital in it. You were so tiny and sweet! It was a very chilly winter day. I had to bundle you tightly and cover most of your face to keep your nose from getting cold. You looked adorable, just like a little mouse peeking out at me! I will never forget that day!" she said.

My mom smiled at me and showed me the picture. It was me, and she was right! I did look like a little mouse. My mom gave me a big hug and said, "Now hurry and change, Mouse. You can come help me make dinner!"

now I finally knew why my mom called me Mouse! It wasn't because I looked like a mouse, was as quiet as a mouse, or loved to eat cheese like a mouse! My mom called me Mouse because she loved me!

The End

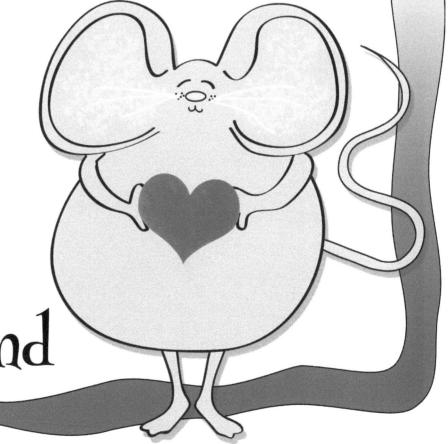

Printed in the USA
CPSIA information can be obtained
at www.ICGtesting.com
JSHW040729190924
69883JS00003B/38